Marie

CW00641210

# Christmas Joy

Spiritual Insights by Chiara Lubich

# Christmas Joy

## Spiritual Insights by Chiara Lubich

New City

London   Edinburgh   Dublin

First published in Italian as
*E torna natale*
© Città Nuova Editrice, Rome

First published in English by
New City
57 Twyford Avenue, London W3 9PZ, England


Translated by Frank Johnson and Callan Slipper
© 1998 New City, London


*Illustrations by Yiannis Hayiannis*
*Cover design by Duncan Harper*


ISBN 0 904287 60 2


British Cataloguing in Publication Data
A catalogue record for this book is available from
the British Library


Scripture quotations are from
the New Revised Version of the Bible


Set in Great Britain by
New City, London

Printed and bound in Great Britain by
The Cromwell Press, Trowbridge, Wiltshire

# CONTENTS

Introduction                                    7

But who is this?                                9

The Trinity has thrown open its gates          12

There is another world                         13

God loves us                                   15

That baby!                                     16

A new order                                    18

My dream                                       20

In their midst                                 21

That baby's dream                              23

Glory to God and peace on earth                26

Echo of the angels' song                       27

What an opportunity!                           28

A mother                                       30

A new light                                    31

What Christmas is for me                        32

The family                                     34

Why Christmas never grows old                    38

They have evicted Jesus                          39

A celebration for everyone                       42

For them                                         45

The promise                                      46

Christmas with those who suffer                  49

The Gospel is for them                           52

To God through other people                      55

Peace                                            58

Every day can be Christmas                       59

Sources                                          61

# INTRODUCTION

The writings in this book have never been published before. They began life as Christmas greetings from the writer, but because of their unique beauty and tremendous depth, many people have felt the desire to see them in book form. Taken together they create a single, though very rich, vision of the mystery of Christmas. Sometimes deceptively simple, they comment upon the many ways in which the birth of God in human form has an impact upon the human race, not, however, in a merely general way. The reader can see how that birth makes a difference to his or her daily life. The wonder of contemplation becomes an invitation to action.

The translators have attempted to render in English the characteristically rhythmic and poetic style of the original. This is not an easy task, but, they say, it was at once a challenge and a joy. The result is a series of prose poems that are in themselves both a challenge and a joy. The attractiveness of the language seeks to entice the reader deeper and deeper into the mystery of Christmas.

There is nothing quite like these writings. They are meditations and, at the same time, a celebration. They can be used as tools to gain greater insight, or they can simply be enjoyed. But however they are treated, they open up a window on to the infinite Love that surrounds us and cares for us.

It is to this Love that the book is dedicated...

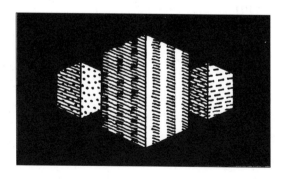

# BUT WHO IS THIS?

And Christmas, like a beautiful poem, comes again:
fir trees,
coloured candles,
snowflakes,
cribs,
seasonal greetings,
people at rest,
midnight Mass...

But who is this,
who is the One who shakes the fibres of every heart,
who, on that night, bends the knees
even of those whose daily lives
find in him little of attraction?
Who is that child calling today,
as in the past,
kings and shepherds,
moving angels and stars?
Who is that new-born child, the weakest of creatures,
son of a girl of fifteen,
who, from a cave, makes the world

feel his presence?
Jesus, it is you, the Son of God!
If you do so much while seeming so little,
it is because you are the All.

You are the All.
And before you, we are nothing.
And yet, since everyone today is exchanging gifts,
allow us to make a gift to you:
we want to give back to you, in our own way, the joy
of returning once more to the world.
For us it is not enough to have Christmas
merely as a time of rejoicing.
We want it to become
a reality – a divine reality.


We know that, if we are united in your name, you are in
    our midst.
So then, here we are, all aflame with the 'goodwill'
    you require;
we recognize one another as brothers and sisters:
men, women, children, skilled workers, labourers,
    politicians, the sick, people who have made a
    name for themselves, people with no name.
We place at your feet everything that is ours, our poor
    scraps, to give fraternal charity the royal place in
    our hearts,
because this is what pleases you and this is why you

came among us.
Here we are, all united...
And you?
You are the God of truth and justice, as well as of love,
and you keep your promises.
Come into our midst, stay with us.
Once the people of your time gave you no welcome. We
        want,
as far as possible,
to remedy that.
We live only to welcome you, to have you in our midst,
        to be not ourselves but you, and to help you build
        on earth the new city, the city of God.

# THE TRINITY
## HAS THROWN OPEN ITS GATES

It is mysterious and momentous
that the second Person of the Most Holy Trinity
became incarnate,
through which, for all eternity, our human nature
is inseparably placed
in the heart of God.
It  is mysterious and goes beyond our reasoning.
God, in his second Person,
will never more be parted from human nature
      in Jesus!

If the Most Holy Trinity has thrown open its gates so
      that the Word
could become human for us,
we are crazy if we do not believe
in the love of God for everyone.

# THERE IS ANOTHER WORLD

'The one who comes from above
is above all;
the one who is of the earth
belongs to the earth
and speaks about earthly things.' (John 3: 31)
That is the difference between Jesus and us.
He comes from on high.
'You came down from the stars...' I have heard sung
     at Christmas.
Jesus brings heaven on earth.
And he speaks about
what he has seen and heard.
There is another world
beyond the one that falls beneath our gaze:
the one from which Jesus came down.
And there
you see and you hear.
We are of the earth.
Herein lies the difference between what we say
and what
'the one who comes from above' says.

His are *eternal words.*
Only one life is spent intelligently:
that of one who,
every day of his or her existence
has the Gospel at heart.
Such a person finds the supreme ideal
in incarnating
the Words of Heaven.

# GOD LOVES US

Christmas, Christmas how many times have we celebrated you with pure joy and unique warmth!

But our hearts are so hardened by the coldness of the world that you could not impress on them your mysterious, incredible message: *God loves us,* one by one and all together.

His love so enveloped us that the blessed Trinity decided to send into our midst, made man, the Son of God. This, so that our brief earthly journey could be lit up, from that very moment, by the Light that never dims

and the absurd death of this life could be transformed into a simple passage to the fuller, the eternal life!

This year at least, Christmas, tell our hearts what you want to say.

We are here:

ready to welcome your voice.

# THAT BABY!

Jesus, when we pray to you in our heart,
when we adore you in the sacred host on the altar,
when we talk to you, present in heaven,
and we thank you for our life,
and we pour out our sorrow to you for our mistakes,
and we ask you for the graces we need,
we think of you always
as adult, as Lord.

Now, with light ever new, Christmas returns every year
and, like a renewed revelation,
you reveal yourself to us as a baby, newly-born, in a
        cradle,
and a wave of emotion invades us.
And we
no longer know how to formulate words,
nor do we dare to ask
for anything,
nor feel that we should burden
such minuscule, albeit almighty, strength.

We are dumbstruck by the mystery,
and the adoring silence of the soul
is fused with the silence of Mary
who, at the declaration of shepherds who had heard
the heavenly singing of angels
'treasured all these words
and pondered them in her heart.' (Luke 2: 19)

Christmas... that baby
always appears to us
as one of the most disconcerting
mysteries of our faith,
because he is the beginning of the revelation
of God's love for us,
which then opens itself out
in all its divine, merciful,
omnipotent majesty.

# A NEW ORDER

When the Word of God became human
he certainly adapted himself
to life in the world
and was baby and child,
man and worker.
But also he brought the way of life
of his heavenly homeland,
and he wanted people and objects
to be recomposed
in a new order,
according
to the law of heaven:
love.

# MY DREAM

This is my 'dream' this Christmas: *a world invaded by love!*

But you will say, 'Jesus came down, as on this night, and the world is still the same; Christians are little more than a billion...'

Yes, but the influence of Christianity in the world is so vast, it is immeasurable. And what is more I believe in his words: 'You will do greater things than I have done.' This is the Gospel.

And so? It may not come in our generation... The important thing is that one day it will come. It will take time, certainly. But we know how to be among the pioneers: if we light a good fire in our midst, the future is predictable: it will burn and triumph.

The important thing is: never extinguish love.

Let us promise this today: a world ablaze with the love of God.

# IN THEIR MIDST

'Where two or three are gathered in my name,
I am there among them.' (Matt. 18: 20)
Among them, just as he was
two thousand years ago
in the midst of Mary and Joseph:
except that his presence, though real,
is a spiritual presence.

Jesus does not like to stay
only in tabernacles.
His wish is to be in the midst of people,
to share with them
thoughts, plans, worries, joys...
This was another reason why he came to earth:
to give us the chance
to have him with us always,
to bring the warmth, the hope, the light, the harmony
that every Christmas contains.

22

# THAT BABY'S DREAM

Christmas,

and the Invisible made itself visible, the Word became flesh, the Uncreated appeared in the created, the Light shone in the darkness.

Given this, it is not without meaning on this day to have the lights, the colours, the presents, the greetings, the cribs, the trees in their finery, the songs, the music...

Nevertheless,

Christmas cannot be reduced to this.

This unique Christian festival must make something flow out of our hearts:

a conviction, a faith without doubts, a striking clarity:

if God came down from heaven for us, there is no doubt that he loves us.

And if someone loves us, if God himself loves us, everything on this earth is easier for us, everything makes more sense: behind the obscure passages of our existence we can read the loving hand of God;

the reasons may often be unknown to us, but they are reasons of love.

Everything can be borne more easily. And everything is more deeply pervaded by joy, if indeed joy is what already we experience.

Because beyond the precious moments in life, like the blossoming of a beautiful love, the birth of a child, a piece of unexpected good fortune, there is a Father's Providence.

Then everything becomes possible.

If you believe, and if you believe in a God who loves us, every impossibility can be shattered, even the impossibility, at times so obvious, for our cradle, this planet that shelters us, to live in peace.

Yes, everything is possible.

In fact, if the All-powerful came among us,
our faith can rise even further.

We can believe, if we hope and ask for it with all our heart, that our world

will start to move towards unity:

to union between generations, between social classes, between races, between Christians divided for centuries, between the faithful of different religions, between peoples.

Unity, an ideal of unity, is in the air in our times.

Many young people in the world believe in it with the
        passion typical of their age and work for this end
        with all their youthful vigour
Let's allow them to dream and to work.
That baby whose birth we are celebrating dreamt
of nothing less.
He came on earth so that all could be one.
And he gave his life
so that his dream could be fulfilled.

# GLORY TO GOD AND PEACE ON EARTH

One prayer certain to be answered
is the one asking for God's glory.
Faith tells us it is so:
God cannot but want it.
And another prayer that God would like to grant,
if all people were to conform to his will,
is peace.
And we are told this by the love
God bears for all his children.
So let us pray this Christmas as well:
'Glory to God in the highest
and peace to people of good will.'

# ECHO OF THE ANGELS' SONG

May these days of Christmas,
days which remind us of Jesus' first appearance on
        earth,
be more than ever
days of profound inner and outer joy,
an echo of the angels' song and of the shepherds'
        gladness!

May we live them so that Jesus,
now ascended into heaven,
when he looks down on earth
and on all the places celebrating his Christmas,
will rest his gaze with particular satisfaction
on the place where we are staying,
so he can admire
a marvellous, living Christmas,
built and re-built, hour by hour,
out of our love for one another,
which makes him really present among us.

# What an opportunity!

St John says: 'To all those who received him,
who believed in his name,
he gave power to become children of God,
who were born,
not of blood or of the will of the flesh or of the will
    of man,
but of God.' (John 1: 12-13)

Perhaps we do not think enough about our destiny
    as Christians.
Perhaps we do not give sufficient witness
to the infinite abyss that exists between a child of God
and a child of the flesh, born of human will.
Perhaps we do not understand
how important it is that in our lives we have
    encountered the Word made flesh,
and that we have believed in him.
It is this believing in him
that makes us children of God.

Herein lies our gratitude
to God for choosing us,
and the responsibility
of transmitting to others
the message of salvation.

# A MOTHER

Christmas: a mother.
His mother.
Our mother.
The law of heaven is to become children again.
Comfort us in your arms, Mary,
so that this Christmas has meaning for us.

# A NEW LIGHT

This year Christmas has a new flavour.

From the birth of the divine infant, from the pure maternity of his immaculate mother, a veil has been removed, a new light has flooded the crib.

Everything is as before, but that mother has an extra beauty; a radiance, perhaps known already by the angels, is admired by our own still enchanted and unwitting eyes.

There where the Babe is born, the Church is born with him.

There where Mary is mother of a child, she is mother of his work: the Church.

The Pope has said: 'Mary as mother of Christ, is also mother of all the faithful and all the pastors, in other words, of the Church.'

# WHAT CHRISTMAS IS FOR ME

Christmas, feast of the birth of Jesus, is for me the reply
      of God and the Church to a need of the soul:
to hear repeated to me every year, through the com-
      memoration of that fact so sweet, so sublime,
so simple and so deep,
that God loves me.

Yes, if in my existence, I am able to fulfil my deepest
      aspirations,
it is only because God has looked also upon me, as he
      has upon everyone, and has become man to give
      me
the laws of life that, like light on the road,
help me walk safely
towards our common destiny.

But Christmas for me is not just a commemoration,
      however meaningful. It is a spur
for me to work to restore the presence of Christ
in the midst of the society in which I live.
He is there where two or more are united in his name

(cf. Matt. 18: 20), like an everyday spiritual
      Christmas,
in homes, in factories, in schools, in public buildings...
This day of Christmas, furthermore, opens my heart to
      the whole of humanity.
Its warmth goes beyond the Christian world
and seems to invade every land,
a sign that that Baby came for everyone.
In fact it is his plan: that all may be one
      (cf. John 17: 21).


And every Christmas then I always ask myself: 'How
      many more Christmases will I see in my life?'
This question, which has no answer, helps me to live
      every year as if it were the last
with a greater awareness of my own Christmas day,
the 'dies natalis',
the day which will signal for me
the beginning of the life that never dies.

# THE FAMILY

Christmas is a celebration of the family.
But where was the most extraordinary family born, but
      in a cave in Bethlehem?
It is there, with the birth of a baby, that it started.
It is there that, for the first time, in the hearts of Mary
and Joseph love was released for a third member: the
      God made man.

The family: it is a word that contains an immense
      meaning: rich, profound, sublime and simple, and
      above all real.
Either the family exists, or it does not.
The atmosphere of a family is an atmosphere of under-
      standing, of calm relaxation,
one of unity, mutual love, peace that affects the mem-
      bers in the whole of their being.

My wish this Christmas would be that one word be
      branded in letters of fire on our souls: family.
A family, whose members starting with a supernatural
      vision, seeing Jesus in others, end with the most

down-to-earth and simple expressions typical of family life.

A family whose members do not have a heart of stone but a heart of flesh, like Jesus, like Mary, like Joseph.

Are there among you some who are suffering because of spiritual trials? They must be understood as much as and more than a mother would. Bring them the light with a word or by example. Do not let them feel the absence of the family warmth, on the contrary, let them feel it all the more.

Are there among you some who are suffering physically? Let them be treated as favourites. It is necessary to suffer with them. Try to understand them right to the depth of their pain.

Are there some who are dying? Imagine yourself in their place and do for them whatever you would have done for you up to the moment of your last breath.

Is one of you rejoicing over some success or for any other reason? Rejoice with him or her so that the joy is not spoilt and the soul closed in on itself, but the happiness is shared by all.

Is one of you going away? Do not let him or her leave without a heart filled with a single legacy: the sense of the family, so as to take it with them wherever they go.

Never put any kind of activity, either spiritual or apostolic, before the spirit of the family.

And wherever you go take Christ's Ideal; you can do nothing better than to try and create, with discretion and prudence, but decisively, the family spirit – a humble spirit, which wants the good of the others, is not proud... it is true, complete, charity.

So, if I had to leave you, I would let Jesus in me repeat: 'Love one another... so that all may be one.'

# Why Christmas never grows old

I think Christmas never grows old,
because it is a deeply human,
as well as a divine mystery.

God, in becoming a human being, raised humanity
to the dizzy heights of the divine,
but at the same time he made it manifest,
disclosing its mystery to people in ecstasy.

Christmas means the warmth of the family,
the amazing phenomenon of motherhood,

the continuity of life through fatherhood.

Christmas means, for the Christian and for humanity –
besides the dawn of the Redemption –
the day in which humanity rediscovers itself, its true
        self,
because it is grafted into God.

# THEY HAVE EVICTED JESUS

It's nearly Christmas and the city streets are covered in lights.

A never-ending row of shops, a sophisticated but exorbitant richness. To the left of our car a row of shop windows catches our attention. Through the window it is snowing gently: an optical illusion. Boys and girls on sledges pulled by reindeer and Disney animals. Still more sledges and Father Christmas and little deer, piglets, hares, frogs, puppets and red dwarfs.

Everything is moving gracefully. Ah! There are the angels... But no! They are fairies, recently invented to adorn the snow-white scene.

A child with his parents stands on tiptoe and watches, fascinated.

But in my heart is disbelief and then, almost, rebellion: this rich world has trapped Christmas and all that goes with it, and has evicted Jesus!

It loves the poetry, the atmosphere, the friendship that Christmas brings, the gifts it suggests, the lights, the stars, the songs. It looks to Christmas for the

best profits of the year. But to Jesus it gives no
thought.

'He came to his own home and his own people received
him not...'

'There was no room for him in the inn...',

no, and not even at Christmas.

Last night I didn't sleep. This thought kept me awake.
If I were to be born again, I would do many
things. I would found a Work at the service of the
Christmases of all people on earth; I would print
the most beautiful cards in the world; I would pro-
duce statues, large and small, of the most taste-
ful art; I would record poems and songs, past and
present; I would illustrate books for children and
adults on this 'mystery of love'; I would write
scripts for plays and films.

I don't know what I would do...

Today I thank the Church for having saved the images.

Years ago, when I was in a country dominated by atheism, a
priest was carving sculptures of angels to remind
people of heaven. Today I understand him better. The
practical atheism, which is now invading the whole
world, demands it. Certainly, keeping Christmas
while banning the New-born causes sadness.

Let us, at least in our own homes, shout out Who is born,
celebrating his coming as never before.

# A CELEBRATION FOR EVERYONE

Over the Christmas period, even in countries gripped by the harshest of winters, a spiritual warmth invades our homes.

As at no other time there is something in the air. An atmosphere which tells of an event. Not everyone talks about it, but everyone feels it. Even people who do not believe in God invent a fable or a character to justify the need they feel to be happy, to rejoice.

Already for weeks – especially in larger towns – streets, shops and houses have been ablaze with lights and festooned with colour.

And then, at Christmas, every heart grows in goodness. The gifts, which many people exchange, are an expression of this.

It is a beautiful custom.

How could we ever think of a year without Christmas? And yet, we notice that something is missing in our society today... also at Christmas.

All these outward things, the songs, the decorations, the parties are not balanced by a profound meditation on what Christmas means. Who are we celebrating? Our children? Ourselves? Who?

Is it not perhaps Jesus, ignored by the majority, rejected by the world, oft-forgotten, who is the focus, the unique and only focus of this great celebration?

Yes, it is he.

And we want to make the figure of Jesus and the contemplation of him emerge above every other kind of display. We want to make his name ring out above every other song, to make his light shine out more than every other outward light.

Jesus, Emmanuel, the God-with-us, explains Christmas.

Yes, because the Son of God, the purest spirit, some two thousand years ago took our flesh, and was born among us, a baby like every other baby.

And he did all of this so that he could share our life, grow, work like us, found the Church, die for our salvation and take us, after this life, to the Life he returned to when he ascended into heaven.

Christmas speaks of the love God has for us.

Baby Jesus is the highest gift that heaven has given to earth, this minuscule earth lost in the immensity of space, among billions of stars, but chosen, chosen to be the dwelling place of the true God become a human being.

Christmas cries out to us that God loves us, that *God is love.*

And we are not genuine Christians if we do not give

Christmas its proper meaning, if we do not know how to extract from this enchanting mystery, surrounded by so many outward things, the truth contained within it.

We must echo the angels who announced the news to the shepherds, and not miss any chance to tell our relatives and friends, our companions, the world, that love has come down to earth for each one of us, that nobody at Christmas should feel alone, abandoned, orphaned, wretched.

Jesus did not come just for one people or another;

God became a human being for the whole of humanity, thus for each one of us.

It is therefore a celebration for everyone, joy for everyone, freedom for everyone, peace for everyone.

# FOR THEM

This Christmas, Lord,
we entrust to you the 'distant' ones,
the many who once were 'near' and who are no longer,
because the evils, the far too many evils of the world,
drove them away from you.
We entrust to you those who do not know you,
but who are searching for you with a pure and sincere heart
and do not know that one day, one sweet, sweet day,
you appeared as a baby on earth.

This Christmas, Lord,
we entrust to you above all those without a faith.
We entrust them to you so that,
on the backdrop of the goodwill they so often display,
a ray of your light may break through,
the star that guides to you may blaze out for an instant,
and they may experience, at least for a few moments,
how full is the joy of those who know you and love you.

We entrust to you the 'distant' ones, Lord,
because we know that it was above all for them
that one day you became a baby.

# THE PROMISE

It is a real joy that year by year the Church offers for
    our consideration the main facts of the life of
    Jesus.
So Christmas comes round year by year and we can
    plunge into the depths of the supremely sweet
    mystery of God become a child.
Jesus, young, beautiful, strong, who launches the
    highest, divine message that the world has ever
    heard or will ever hear,
Jesus who, to pay in person for his own cause, dies,
today makes us think of him and admire him as small,
    weak, poor,
next to a mother who was unknown then and still very
    young
and a father who stands in for his heavenly Father.

The crib scene inspires such tenderness, it is so true, so
    rich in meaning, the incarnation of the beatitudes,
and it touches some of the strings of our hearts which
    are normally silent

because the everyday din of many and weighty problems
prevents us perceiving their sound.
But at least on Christmas Day let us make space for this
exquisite harmony
which is echoed in the tremendous, the endless silences
of the world's poor,
those who are often struck by catastrophes that take
your breath away, the sick, the children who
belong to no one, those dying on the streets of
India, the disinherited, those without motivation
because without work,
all of the wretched who are loved by Jesus because they
are like him right from the very moment of his
birth.

We too must love them,
and may our hearts, on this Christmas Day,
choose them again as the most favoured ones of all.
They await us in our cities, they await us in every country and continent...

This promise before the Child
is the best way
in which we can spend
our Christmas.

# CHRISTMAS WITH THOSE WHO SUFFER

The warmth of Christmas leads us to feel more like a
      family, more one among us, more brothers and
      sisters,
to share everything: joys and sufferings –
above all to share the sufferings of those who, for many
      different reasons, are spending this Christmas
      face to face with pain.
It is to people like this that we wish to turn in a special
      way.
Suffering!
The pain that sometimes takes hold of us completely or
      the pain that grazes us and mixes bitter with
      sweet in our daily lives.
Suffering: an illness, a misfortune, a trial, a painful
      event...
Suffering!
How should we view this thing which directly concerns
      many people at the moment, or which is always
      ready to appear in everyone's life?
How can we define it, how can we identify it? What name
      can we give it? Whose voice is it?

If we look at suffering with human eyes we are tempted to seek its cause either inside or outside of ourselves, in human malice for example, or in nature, or in something else...

That accident was so and so's fault; that illness is my fault; that painful trial can be traced back to such and such...

And all of this may also be true, but if we reason only in this way, we forget something more. We forget that behind the plot of our lives is God with his love, who wants or allows everything for a higher reason: our good.

Suffering, for whoever looks at it from the Christian perspective, is something great; it is, in fact, the possibility of completing Christ's passion in ourselves, for our own purification and for the redemption of many.

What can we say, today, to someone struggling with suffering? What can we wish them? How should we behave with them?

First of all we should approach them with the greatest respect. Even though they do not perhaps think it, in these moments they are being visited by God.

Then let us, as far as is possible, share their crosses with them. Let us assure them that they are always in our thoughts and in our prayers, so that they know how to take directly from God's hands all that troubles them and makes them suffer, uniting

it to Jesus' passion, for like that it will reach its
full potential.
And let us remind them of that marvellous Christian
principle, whereby a suffering, loved as the face
of Jesus crucified and forsaken, can be transformed
into joy.

This Christmas let us wish that all may know how to
welcome with love, with great love, the great or small
suffering they encounter, and give it to the baby
Jesus who is born today, just as the wise
men offered their gifts.
It will be the best frankincense, the best gold, the best
myrrh
we could possibly bring to the crib.

# THE GOSPEL IS FOR THEM

It is Christmas and never as this year have I waited for
    it with such joy;
but it was not a matter of waiting,
it has been a continuous Christmas celebration!

What counts is love, true love...
that love which we have learnt to have in our hearts,
never turning our gaze from Jesus crucified and forsaken.
Here lies the secret of unity,
the rebirth of our souls
and, perhaps, of the world.

May Jesus forsaken be reborn, in this night,
shining in our hearts
as the only star of our life (cf. Mark 15: 34).
May God close our eyes to everything
to keep them open only on him.
Let us ask this one grace for each and everyone:
to love him for the whole of our existence,
so that God may make it blaze a trail of light,
be a witness of God.

And this is all. This is sufficient.
Let us love him in ourselves, in the infinite nuances of
    our sufferings,
but let us love him above all outside ourselves,
in our brothers and sisters,
in all our brothers and sisters.
And if, among them, we can have any preference, let us
    love him in the most wretched,
in the most run down, the most revolting, the most
    rejected, the most racked by agony,
the refuse of society.
Jesus said he came 'to bring good news to the poor'
    (Luke 4: 18). May this become a byword for us.
It is for them above all that the Gospel promises the
    beatitudes:
those who weep, those who hunger, those who are per-
    secuted...
Let us concentrate on them:
they are the Lord's favourites!
May they become our favourites.

Let us give ourselves without measure,
seeking and finding the face of the Forsaken One among
    us and around us.
And this Christmas let us ask that love be born in us
to such an extent that we each become
'another Jesus', all of us the 'living' Church, other
    'Marys',

53

become so much Mary that suffering humanity can
repeat of us
'Refuge of sinners', 'Consoler of the afflicted', 'Help of
Christians'.
This is our prayer tonight.

# To God through other people

Christmas is drawing nearer, the Lord is about to arrive,
and the liturgy invites us to prepare the road for
him: 'Prepare the way of the Lord, make his paths
straight' (Mark 1: 3).

ι He, who entered history two thousand years ago, wants ι ←
to enter our lives, but the road in us is cluttered
by obstacles. We need to flatten the hills, remove
the blocks. What are the obstacles that can obstruct
the road for Jesus?

They are all the desires not in conformity with God's
will that well up in our soul; they are the attach-
ments that cling to it;

minuscule desires to speak or keep silent, when we
ought to do the opposite;

desires for affirmation, for respect, for affection; desires
for things, for health, for life... when God does
not want them;

the more evil desires, of rebellion, judgement, revenge...

They all well up in our soul and invade it completely.

We have to extinguish these desires decisively, remove
these obstacles, put ourselves back in God's will

and so prepare the way of the Lord.

We must, the Word says, make his paths straight.

To make them straight: exactly that. Our desires lead us off the path. If we extinguish them, we put ourselves back on the ray of God's will and we find our road again.

But there is a method of being sure of walking on a straight way, which takes us with certainty to our goal: to God.

It has an obligatory route; it is called *our neighbour.*

This Christmas, let us throw ourselves once again into loving every person we meet during the day.

Let us light up in our hearts that most ardent and praiseworthy desire which God most certainly wants: the desire to love every neighbour, making ourselves one with him or her in everything, with a love that is without self-interest and without limits.

Love will revive relationships and persons and will not allow selfish desires to spring up. In fact, it is the best antidote to selfishness.

We could prepare for Christmas like this, as a gift for Jesus who comes, giving him this as our fruit: rich and succulent; and our hearts: enflamed, consumed by love.

# PEACE

Jesus comes back as a baby
to tell us that God
is not far away.

The angels are still singing:
peace on earth
to people he loves.

Let us ask your defenceless omnipotence
to bend down and to snuff out the arrogance of
        violence,
to remove hatred from all hearts
and to put love there,
to make it so that soon no nation in the world
will remember
what war is.

# EVERY DAY CAN BE CHRISTMAS

It's Christmas!
The Word became a human being and set love alight on
        earth.

It's Christmas!
And we would never wish the sun to set on this day.
Teach us, O Lord, how to preserve your presence
        among us.

It's Christmas!
Let your love, set alight on earth, burn our hearts and
        let us love one another as you desire!
Then you will be there among us.
And every day, if we love one another,
        can be Christmas.

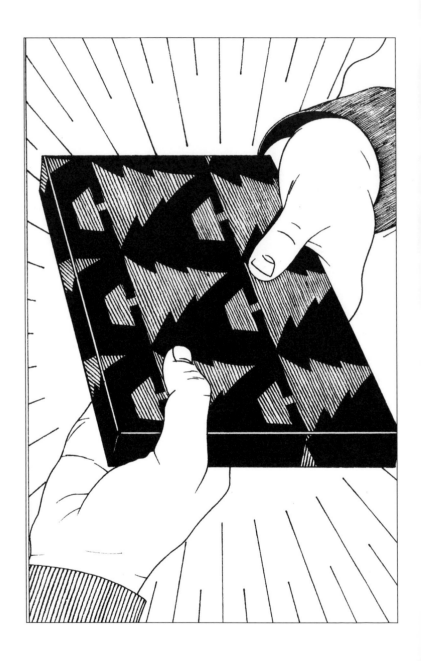

# Sources

The prose poems in this book, now published for the first time, began as Christmas greetings on the following dates:

| | | |
|---|---|---|
| *Christmas 1954* | The Gospel is for them | 52 |
| *20 December 1957* | But who is this? | 9 |
| *Christmas 1962* | The Trinity has thrown open its gates | 12 |
| *Christmas 1963* | Why Christmas never grows old | 38 |
| *Christmas 1964* | A new light | 31 |
| *Christmas 1966* | Glory to God and peace on earth | 26 |
| *November 1968* | There is another world | 13 |
| *5 December 1968* | That baby! | 16 |
| *Christmas 1968* | What an opportunity! | 28 |
| *Christmas 1972* | A mother | 30 |
| *3 December 1973* | What Christmas is for me | 32 |
| *Christmas 1973* | The family | 34 |
| *Christmas 1974* | In their midst | 21 |
| *Christmas 1975* | God loves us | 15 |
| *Christmas 1976* | The promise | 46 |
| *Christmas 1979* | A celebration for everyone | 42 |
| *Christmas 1980* | They have evicted Jesus | 39 |
| *Christmas 1982* | Every day can be Christmas | 59 |

| | | |
|---|---|---|
| *Christmas 1983* | For them | 45 |
| *Christmas 1984* | Echo of the angels' song | 27 |
| *Christmas 1985* | That baby's dream | 23 |
| *Christmas 1986* | Christmas with those who suffer | 49 |
| *Christmas 1988* | My dream | 20 |
| *Christmas 1990* | Peace | 58 |
| *Christmas 1991* | A new order | 18 |
| *Christmas 1994* | To God through other people | 55 |